macOS® Keyboard Shortcuts

TEACHUCOMP, INC.®
...it's all about you

KEY: ⌘ = Command   ^ = Control   ⏏ = Media Eject   ▦ = Mission Control   ⌥ = Option   ⏻ = Power   ⇧ = Shift

Common

Character Viewer (Emoji, Symbols)	^ ⌘ SPACE
Close active window	⌘ W
Close all windows in app	⌥ ⌘ W
Copy selected item	⌘ C
Create new folder in Finder	⇧ ⌘ N
Cut selection	⌘ X
Find	⌘ F
Find next	⌘ G
Find previous	⇧ ⌘ G
Force quit app	⌥ ⌘ ESC
Hide all but active app	⌥ ⌘ H
Hide windows of active app	⌘ H
Minimize active window to Dock	⌘ M
Minimize all windows of active app	⌥ ⌘ M
Open new tab	⌘ T
Open preferences for active app	⌘ , (Comma)
Open selected item	⌘ O
Paste Clipboard contents	⌘ V
Print current document	⌘ P
Redo previous undo command	⇧ ⌘ Z
Save current document	⌘ S
Screenshot: Capture and Record	⇧ ⌘ 5
Screenshot: Full Screen	⇧ ⌘ 3
Screenshot: Select Area	⇧ ⌘ 4
Select all items	⌘ A
Show/hide Spotlight search field	⌘ SPACE
Spotlight Search from Finder	⌘ ⌥ SPACE
Switch between open apps	⌘ TAB
Undo previous command	⌘ Z
Use app in full screen, if supported	^ ⌘ F
Use Quick Look on selected item	SPACE

Documents

Align Center	⇧ ⌘ | (Vertical Bar)
Align Left	⇧ ⌘ {
Align Right	⇧ ⌘ }
Boldface selected text, or turn on/off	⌘ B
Center cursor or selection in visible area	^ L
Copy Style: Copy formatting settings	⌥ ⌘ C
Delete character to left of insertion point	^ H
Delete character to right of insertion point	^ D
Delete insertion pt. to end of line/paragraph	^ K
Delete word to left of insertion point	⌥ DEL
Extend selection one character left	⇧ ←
Extend selection one character right	⇧ →
Extend selection to end of paragraph	⌥ ⇧ ↓
Extend selection to end of word	⌥ ⇧ →
Extend selection to start of paragraph	⌥ ⇧ ↑
Extend selection to start of word	⌥ ⇧ ←
Help menu	⇧ ⌘ ?
Insert new line after insertion point	^ O
Insert web link	⌘ K
Italicize selected text, or turn on/off	⌘ I
Move down one line	^ N
Move insertion point to end of document	⌘ ↓
Move insertion point to end of line	⌘ →
Move insertion point to end of next word	⌥ →
Move insertion point to start of document	⌘ ↑
Move insertion point to start of line	⌘ ←
Move insertion pt. to start of previous word	⌥ ←
Move one character backward	^ B
Move one character forward	^ F
Move to start of line or paragraph	^ A
Move to end of line or paragraph	^ E
Move up one line	^ P
Page Down: Scroll down one page	Fn ↓
Page setup window	⇧ ⌘ P
Page Up: Scroll up one page	Fn ↑
Paste & Match surrounding style	⌥ ⇧ ⌘ V
Paste Style: Apply copied style	⌥ ⌘ V
Save As dialog or Duplicate document	⇧ ⌘ S
Scroll to start of document	Fn ←
Scroll to end of document	Fn →
Select Desktop folder in dialog box	⌘ D
Select Search field in dialog box	⌥ ⌘ F
Select text: Insertion pt. to end of doc	⇧ ⌘ ↓
Select text: Insertion pt. to end of line	⇧ ⌘ →
Select text: Insertion pt. to start of doc	⇧ ⌘ ↑
Select text: Insertion pt. to start of line	⇧ ⌘ ←
Sho	⌘ D
Sho	⌘ T
Sho	⌘ I
Show	⌘ T
Size: Decrease size of selected item	⇧ ⌘ -
Size: Increase size of selected item	⇧ ⌘ +
Spellcheck	⌘ ; (Semicolon)
Spelling and Grammar window	⇧ ⌘ : (Colon)
Swap characters on each side of insertion pt.	^ T
Underline selected text, or turn on/off	⌘ U

Finder and System

Add selected Finder item to Dock	^ ⇧ ⌘ T
Add selected item to sidebar	^ ⌘ T
Adjust display brightness in steps	⌥ ⇧ 🔅 or 🔆
Adjust keyboard brightness in steps	⌥ ⇧ 🔅 or 🔆
Adjust sound volume in steps	⌥ ⇧ 🔉 or 🔊
Close selected folder (list view only)	←
Copy dragged item	⌥ (Hold and drag)
Create new folder	⇧ ⌘ N
Create new folder with selection	^ ⌘ N
Duplicate selected files	⌘ D
Eject selected disk or volume	⌘ E
Empty Trash	⇧ ⌘ DEL
Empty Trash without confirmation	⌥ ⇧ ⌘ DEL
Go to next folder	⌘]
Go to previous folder	⌘ [
Make alias of dragged item	⌥ ⌘ (Hold and drag)
Make alias of selected item	^ ⌘ A
Move Clipboard files to current location	⌥ ⌘ V
Move item to different volume	⌘ (Hold and drag)
Open AirDrop window	⇧ ⌘ R
Open Computer window	⇧ ⌘ C
Open Connect to Server window	⌘ K

TeachUcomp, Inc.
Computer Software Training & Continuing Education.

www.teachucomp.com
info@teachucomp.com
877.925.8080

Finder and System *Continued*

Action	Shortcut
Open Desktop folder	⇧ ⌘ D
Open Display preferences	⌥ [Brightness]
Open Documents folder	⇧ ⌘ O
Open Downloads folder	⌥ ⌘ L
Open folder in separate tab/window	⌘ Double-click
Open folder that contains current folder	⌘ ↑
Open Go to Folder window	⇧ ⌘ G
Open Home folder	⇧ ⌘ H
Open iCloud Drive	⇧ ⌘ I
Open Keyboard preferences	⌥ [Keyboard brightness]
Open Mission Control preferences	⌥ [Mission Control]
Open Network window	⇧ ⌘ K
Open new Finder window	⌘ N
Open Recents window	⇧ ⌘ F
Open selected folder (list view only)	→
Open selected item	⌘ ↓
Open selected item in new window	⌥ Double-click
Open Sound preferences	⌥ [Volume]
Open Utilities folder	⇧ ⌘ U
Quick Look: preview selected files	⌘ Y
Quick Look: slideshow of selected files	⌥ ⌘ Y
Show all windows of active app	⌃ ↓
Show desktop	⌘ [Mission Control]
Show Get Info window for selected file	⌘ I
Show next tab in Finder	⌃ TAB
Show original file for selected alias	⌘ R
Show previous tab in Finder	⌃ ⇧ TAB
Show View Options	⌘ J
Show/hide Dock	⌥ ⌘ D
Show/hide path bar in Finder	⌥ ⌘ P
Show/hide Preview pane in Finder	⇧ ⌘ P
Show/hide Sidebar in Finder	⌥ ⌘ S
Show/hide status bar in Finder	⌘ /
Show/hide tab bar when single tab open	⇧ ⌘ T
Show/hide toolbar when single tab open	⌥ ⌘ T
Spotlight search in Finder	⌘ F
Trash selected item	⌘ DEL
Turn video mirroring on or off	⌘ [Brightness]
View folders that contain current folder	⌘ Click window Title Bar
View items in Finder as icons	⌘ 1
View items in Finder as list	⌘ 2
View items in Finder in columns	⌘ 3
View items in Finder in a gallery	⌘ 4

Safari

Bookmarks

Action	Shortcut
Add bookmark	⌘ D
Delete bookmark	Drag bookmark off top of Favorites bar
Move bookmark	Drag bookmark left or right on Favorites bar
Open all bookmarks from a folder	⌘ Click folder in Favorites bar

Bookmarks Sidebar/Bookmarks View

Action	Shortcut
Change bookmark name/address	Select bookmark, press return
Close selected folder	←
Create folder of selected bookmarks/folders	⌥ Click New Folder
Delete bookmark	⌃ Click bookmark, then select Delete
Finish editing bookmark name	RETURN
Open selected bookmark	SPACE
Open selected folder	→
Select bookmarks/folders in sidebar	⌘ Click
Select next bookmark or folder	↑ or ↓
Show/hide Bookmarks sidebar	⌃ ⌘ 1

Current Webpage

Action	Shortcut
Copy selected item	⌘ C
Highlight next field or menu	TAB
Highlight next field, menu, or clickable item	⌥ TAB
Paste most recently copied item	⌘ V
Print current webpage	⌘ P
Search current webpage	⌘ F
Select Smart Search field	⌘ L

Downloads

Action	Shortcut
Download linked file	⌥ Click a link to the file
Open downloaded file	Double-click the file in the downloads list

History

Action	Shortcut
Go back to previous webpage	⌘ [
Go forward to next webpage	⌘]
View recently visited by name	Click & hold Back or Forward button for list
View recently visited by URL	⌥ Click & hold Back or Forward button

Preferences

Action	Shortcut
Change Safari preferences	⌘ , (Comma)
Go to homepage	⇧ ⌘ H

Reading List

Action	Shortcut
Add current page	⇧ ⌘ D
Add linked page	⇧ Click a link to the page
Close Reader	ESC
Open Reader	⇧ ⌘ R
Remove page	⌃ Click page summary in sidebar, choose Remove Item
Show/hide Reading List sidebar	⌃ ⌘ 2

Scroll

Action	Shortcut
Scroll down a screen	SPACE
Scroll in larger increments	⌥ ↑ ↓ ← →
Scroll up a screen	⇧ SPACE
Scroll up, down, left, or right	↑ ↓ ← →

Tabs

Action	Shortcut
Close active tab	⌘ W
Close all tabs except one	⌥ Click Close button on tab to keep open
Go to next tab	⇧ ⌘]
Go to previous tab	⇧ ⌘ [
Open page in new tab	⌘ Click link or bookmark
Open page in new tab/make active	⇧ ⌘ Click link or bookmark
Reopen last tab closed	⇧ ⌘ T
Select one of your first nine tabs	⌘ 1...9
Show tab overview	⇧ ⌘ \

Window

Action	Shortcut
Reopen last window closed	⇧ ⌘ T
Switch to another Safari window	⌘ ` (Grave accent-above Tab key)

Zoom

Action	Shortcut
Reset Zoom	⌘ 0
Zoom website content	⌘ + or −
Zoom website text	⌥ ⌘ + or −

Sleep, Log Out, and Shut Down*

Action	Shortcut
Force restart (no saving)**	⌃ ⌘ ⏻
Force Shut Down	⏻ (Press and hold)
Lock screen	⌃ ⌘ Q
Log out	⇧ ⌘ Q
Log out (no confirmation)	⌥ ⇧ ⌘ Q
Put displays to sleep**	⌃ ⇧ ⏻ or ⏏
Put Mac to sleep**	⌥ ⌘ ⏻ or ⏏
Quit all apps and restart	⌃ ⌘ ⏏
Quit all apps and shut down**	⌃ ⌥ ⌘ ⏻ or ⏏
Restart, sleep, or shut down dialog**	⌃ ⏻ or ⏏
Turn on/off or wake from sleep	⏻

**May need to press and hold longer than other shortcuts*
***Does not apply to the Touch ID sensor*

ISBN 978-1-958446-09-6